# APATOSAURUS

by Janet Riehecky
illustrated by Lydia Halverson

THE CHILD'S WORLD

MANKATO, MN

*Grateful appreciation is expressed to Bret S. Beall,*
*Curatorial Coordinator for the Department of Geology,*
*Field Museum of Natural History, Chicago, Illinois,*
*who reviewed this book to insure its accuracy.*

PAPERBACK EDITION
ISBN 0-516-46277-6

**Library of Congress Cataloging in Publication Data**

Riehecky, Janet, 1953-
  Apatosaurus / by Janet Riehecky ; illustrated by Lydia Halverson.
  p. cm. — (Dinosaurs)
  Summary: Describes the physical characteristics and probable
behavior of the huge dinosaur whose name means "deceptive lizard."
  ISBN 0-89565-423-7
  1. Apatosaurus—Juvenile literature.   [1. Apatosaurus.
2. Dinosaurs.]   I. Halverson, Lydia, ill.   II. Title.   III. Series:
Riehecky, Janet, 1953-       Dinosaurs.
QE862.S3R53    1988
567.9'7—dc19                                        88-1694
                                                      CIP
                                                      AC

# APATOSAURUS

Long before people lived on earth, dinosaurs ruled the world.

There are many things we still don't know about the dinosaurs. We may never find some of those things out. But it can be fun to look at dinosaurs in museums, or read about them in a book, or even dream about them at night.

 ## Dinosaur Fun

Whoever finds the bones of a dinosaur first is entitled to give that dinosaur its name. Scientists try to give dinosaurs names that describe them. For instance, Triceratops means "three-horned face," and Tyrannosaurus means "tyrant lizard." You can play a "Name the Dinosaur" game.

Make dinosaur bones out of paper or clay. Hide them in your house or yard. Then have your friends search for them. Whenever someone finds a bone, he gets to make up a name for his "dinosaur." Here is a list of some of the names scientists have used to describe dinosaurs:

proto means *first*

tri means *three*

don means *tooth*

saurus means *lizard*

mega means *big*

ornitho means *bird-like*

mono means *one*

deino means *terrible*

raptor means *thief*

tarbo means *alarming*

nodo means *lumpy*

nano means *small*

There were as many different dinosaurs then as there are different animals in the zoo today.

Some dinosaurs had horns and frills.

Others had armor-plated bodies.

There were gentle giants, which peacefully ate different plants, . . .

and ferocious meat eaters that attacked
and killed other animals for food.

One of the gentle giants was the Apatosaurus (ah-PAT-uh-sawr-us). Its name means "deceptive lizard," which is a good name because it "deceived" scientists for a long time.

For many years scientists thought there were two different kinds of dinosaurs—the Apatosaurus and the Brontosaurus. Then they found out they were the same. Because Apatosaurus was the name this dinosaur was given first, that is its correct name.

elevated nostrils

small, narrow head

peglike teeth

long, flexible neck

tough, leathery skin with
many folds and wrinkles

front feet rounded and
padded like an elephant's

legs as thick as tree trunks

one large inner claw

back feet also
rounded and padded

three claws slanted outward

The Apatosaurus was not the biggest dinosaur to live, but close to it. It often grew to more than seventy feet long, and it weighed more than thirty tons—that's bigger than seven elephants put together!

Its back legs were longer than its front legs, which gave its back a long, sweeping curve. At its hips it was fifteen feet tall, and its neck added another fifteen feet. So if it were living today, it could stretch its neck up high enough to look in a second-story window—without standing on its tiptoes!

*long, whiplike tail*

The Apatosaurus was so big it needed two "brains"! The real one, in its head, was for thinking. It was only about as big as a person's fist and weighed less than a pound. That meant the Apatosaurus probably wasn't very smart, though scientists don't know for sure.

The second one was a "nerve center" near the hips. This wasn't really a second brain. It was a control center for the tail and back legs of the gigantic creature. After all, what if somebody stepped on its tail? It wouldn't want to wait for a message to get seventy feet to its head before it could move out of the way!

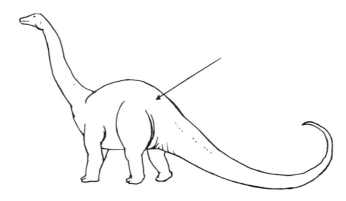

The Apatosaurus was big, but it was gentle. It left other dinosaurs alone as long as they let it do what it wanted to do—and what it wanted to do was eat! It took a lot of food to fill up something that big.

The Apatosaurus spent almost all day, every day, eating. It ate plants from the lakes and swamps. It ate moss and ferns. But what it especially liked were the leaves on the tops of the trees. And if a tree was too tall, the Apatosaurus just knocked it down.

The Apatosaurus swallowed almost everything in its path—sometimes even rocks! The rocks weren't for food, though. They were to help grind up the plants that the Apatosaurus had eaten. The Apatosaurus had only a few, small, peglike teeth, which weren't very good for chewing. The rocks in the Apatosaurus' stomach broke up the plants so they could be digested.

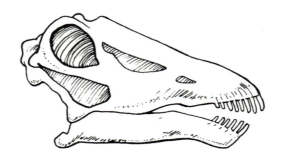

The Apatosaurus was so big it didn't need to be afraid of most things, but there were dangers in its world. The Apatosaurus' huge size made it difficult for it to stop suddenly—and that was a problem if it came upon a cliff unexpectedly.

And its huge size was not always enough to stop a hungry Allosaurus from attacking it, if the Apatosaurus was caught alone or already injured.

However, the Apatosaurus was not defenseless. It could use its huge body to

crush a smaller enemy, or lash at the enemy with its thick, muscular tail. And if it needed to get away, it could wade into very deep water and still keep its head above water.

But the Apatosaurus didn't only go into the water when it was chased in. In the heat of the day, an Apatosaurus would plunge into a cool lake to escape the heat with a nice swim. And at any time of the day the water could help to support the gigantic weight of the Apatosaurus, giving its legs a rest.

Scientists aren't sure how Apatosaurs had babies. Some scientists think the Apatosaurs bore their children alive. These scientists think a mother took care of its baby until it was big enough to take care of itself.

Others think the mother laid many eggs in a nest dug in a sandy cove. The Apatosaurus would leave the nest after laying the eggs, and the babies would be on their own after they hatched. They would have to find their own food, and hide from meat-eating dinosaurs until they were old enough to join a herd.

Someday maybe scientists will find either the fossils of a pregnant Apatosaurus or Apatosaurus eggs. Then we will know for sure which of these ideas is right.

The Apatosaurus was a social creature. It preferred to travel in groups of perhaps two dozen. These herds would roam the countryside, going from the swamps to the dry land, and back again, seeking food.

The little Apatosaurs would be grouped in the center of a herd, with the big ones forming a protective wall around them. It was up to the little ones, though, to keep up. If they fell behind, the adults wouldn't wait.

These herds might cover five miles in a day—and there was never any doubt where they had been. All the plants would be stripped and everything would be trampled down—as if a herd of bulldozers had come through.

There are some scientists who think this may have helped kill off the Apatosaurs and other big dinosaurs. They think these dinosaurs ate plants faster than new ones could grow. Without enough food, they couldn't survive.

No one knows if this is what happened, but we do know that the Apatosaurus and most of the other "gentle giants" all died long before the end of the Age of Dinosaurs.

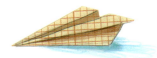

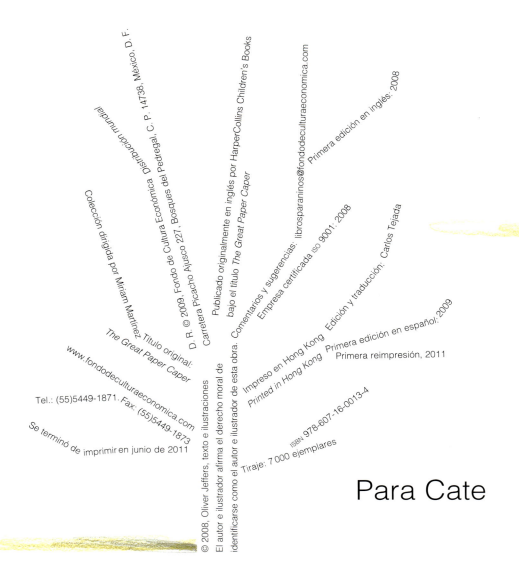

Colección dirigida por Miriam Martínez

The Great Paper Caper

www.fondodeculturaeconomica.com

Tel.: (55)5449-1871. Fax: (55)5449-1873

Se terminó de imprimir en junio de 2011

Título original:

Distribución mundial

D. R. © 2009, Fondo de Cultura Económica

Carretera Picacho Ajusco 227, Bosques del Pedregal, C. P. 14738, México, D. F.

Publicado originalmente en inglés por HarperCollins Children's Books
bajo el título The Great Paper Caper

Comentarios y sugerencias: librosparaninos@fondodeculturaeconomica.com

Empresa certificada ISO 9001: 2008

Primera edición en inglés: 2008

© 2008, Oliver Jeffers, texto e ilustraciones
El autor e ilustrador afirma el derecho moral de
identificarse como el autor e ilustrador de esta obra.

Impreso en Hong Kong  Edición y traducción: Carlos Tejada
Printed in Hong Kong  Primera edición en español: 2009
Primera reimpresión, 2011

ISBN 978-607-16-0013-4

Tiraje: 7 000 ejemplares

Para Cate

Jeffers, Oliver
    El misterioso caso del oso / Oliver Jeffers ; trad. de Carlos Tejada. —
México : FCE, 2008
    [40] p. : ilus. ; 28 x 22 cm — (Colec. Los Especiales de A la Orilla
del Viento)
    ISBN 978-607-16-0013-4

    1. Literatura Infantil I. Tejada, Carlos, tr. II. Ser. III. t.

LC PZ7                                    Dewey 808.068 J754m

# El Misterioso
# caso del OSO

LOS ESPECIALES DE
*A la orilla del viento*
FONDO DE CULTURA ECONÓMICA
MÉXICO

Hubo una época en el bosque...

en la que no todo era como debía ser.

Los que vivían ahí empezaron a notar cosas extrañas.
Todos estaban de acuerdo en que las ramas no deberían desaparecer de
los árboles así como así.

Alguien —volvieron a coincidir— se las debía de estar robando; y comenzaron a echarse la culpa entre ellos.

Pero todos tenían una coartada sólida para probar su inocencia.
Ellos no podían haberlo hecho. El ladrón debía de ser alguien más...

Todo era muy misterioso.

Entonces se inició una pesquisa para llegar al fondo del asunto.

A cada uno se le asignó una tarea para descubrir la identidad del ladrón.

Yo seré el detective y tú puedes ser el juez

¿POR QUÉ tengo que ser el juez?

¿Por qué no él?

Porque yo soy el fiscal

Sacaron fotografías, tomaron notas y examinaron cada hoja detenidamente.

Pero, a pesar de su minuciosa investigación, no encontraron pistas.

Entonces, la declaración de un testigo los condujo a una
evidencia que había aterrizado no muy lejos de allí.

Y que tenía huellas de oso por todas partes.

Habían encontrado al culpable.

Detuvieron al oso y lo fotografiaron.

Lo interrogaron hasta altas horas de la noche.

Al día siguiente, el oso confesó todo...

Habló sobre el campeonato de aviones de papel y lo desesperado que estaba por ganar... él sabía que no era muy bueno y se le había acabado el papel y no tenía a quién pedir ayuda. No había querido hacer ningún daño y estaba arrepentido por haber cortado los árboles sin pedir permiso.

Mmmh, no está mal, pensaron todos. Pero tendrá que reparar el daño
sembrando más árboles...
¿Un campeonato de aviones de papel, eh? Suena interesante.

El oso cumplió su palabra. Al mismo tiempo, y mientras recogían los aviones de papel, los demás tuvieron una idea...

Juntaron todos los avioncitos e hicieron uno nuevo.

# Aviones de PAPEL. Instrucciones avanzadas

TV GUÍA PARA la EXCELENCIA AERONÁUTICA

MODELO  Nº 38

EL PODEROSO CÓNDOR

Una aeronave intimidante y ENCANTADORA que cortará el aire como MANTEQUILLA

PASOS :

① Use un pedazo de papel que tenga 4 lados

② Haga todos los dobleces y demás cosas

③ la parte DIFÍCIL

④ mmm... la parte REALMENTE difícil

⑤ Observe

⑥ Cómo se debe ver

OPCIONES PARA EL DESPEGUE

Se requiere tomar vuelo